MW01428709

HORSING AROUND

QUARTER HORSES

By Barbara M. Linde

Gareth Stevens
Publishing

Please visit our website, www.garethstevens.com. For a free color catalog of all our high-quality books, call toll free 1-800-542-2595 or fax 1-877-542-2596.

A special thanks to Patricia Howell of Merry Mount Farms in Toano, Virginia, and Suzanne Thiele-Thornton of Felicity Arabians in Carrollton, Virginia, for their time and knowledge.

Library of Congress Cataloging-in-Publication Data

Linde, Barbara M.
 Quarter horses / Barbara M. Linde.
     p. cm. — (Horsing around)
 Includes index.
 ISBN 978-1-4339-6470-1 (pbk.)
 ISBN 978-1-4339-6471-8 (6-pack)
 ISBN 978-1-4339-6468-8 (library binding)
 1. Quarter horse—Juvenile literature. I. Title.
 SF293.Q3L48 2012
 636.133—dc23

                                                20110274

First Edition

Published in 2012 by
Gareth Stevens Publishing
111 East 14th Street, Suite 349
New York, NY 10003

Copyright © 2012 Gareth Stevens Publishing

Designer: Michael J. Flynn
Editor: Therese Shea

Photo credits: Cover, (front cover, back cover, p. 1 wooden sign), (front cover, back cover, pp. 2–4, 7–8, 11–12, 15–16, 19–24 wood background), pp. 1, 5, 6, 14, 17, 18, 20 Shutterstock.com; p. 9 SuperStock/Getty Images; p. 10 MPI/Archive Photos/Getty Images; p. 13 iStockphoto.com.

All rights reserved. No part of this book may be reproduced in any form without permission in writing from the publisher, except by a reviewer.

Printed in the United States of America

CPSIA compliance information: Batch #CW12GS: For further information contact Gareth Stevens, New York, New York at 1-800-542-2595.

Contents

What Is a Quarter Horse? 4

Special Features 7

A Horse for the Colonists. 8

A Horse for the Pioneers 11

A Modern Work Horse. 12

A Racing Horse 15

Quarter Horses for Fun 16

Quarter Horses in the Movies 19

Keeping Quarter Horses Healthy. 20

Glossary 22

For More Information. 23

Index 24

Words in the glossary appear in **bold** type the first time they are used in the text.

What Is a Quarter Horse?

Have you seen a horse with large muscles and a broad chest zipping through a field at full speed? It was probably an American quarter horse!

This **breed** is usually between 14 and 16 **hands** high at its withers, or shoulders. This is between 56 and 64 inches (142 and 163 cm) tall. Quarter horses often weigh around 1,100 pounds (500 kg).

Quarter horses are smart, gentle, and strong. They're one of the fastest and most popular breeds in the world.

THE MANE FACT

Quarter horses usually live between 20 and 40 years.

The official name of the quarter horse breed is American quarter horse.

This is a sorrel-colored colt. Notice the white markings on the back legs and face.

6

Special Features

A quarter horse has a small head with a wide mouth. There are two different body types. The stock horse is shorter, with a heavy-looking, powerful body. The racing horse is taller and sleeker. Both types move quickly.

Quarter-horse coats may be one of 17 different colors, including chestnut, black, and gray. The most valued quarter horses have solid coats, but some are born with white markings.

THE MANE FACT

Some other quarter-horse colors are dun (brownish gray), buckskin (grayish yellow), palomino (golden), and cremello (cream).

A Horse for the Colonists

British colonists brought horses to Virginia starting in 1610. Soon, they began breeding their horses with the faster horses of the Chickasaw Indians. When racing, these horses could **sprint** quickly down village roads. This new breed was called the quarter horse because these races were usually a quarter mile (0.4 km) long.

In the mid-1700s, some Virginia farmers began breeding Thoroughbred **stallions** from England with colonial **mares**. The horses that were born were even faster than other quarter horses.

The colonists used quarter horses for plowing fields, pulling logs and carts, and riding.

In the 1860s, the Pony Express often used quarter horses for their mail delivery service.

10

A Horse for the Pioneers

In the late 1700s, quarter horses began to travel west with the **pioneers**. These sturdy horses pulled heavy wagons across the Great Plains to Texas, California, and other areas.

By the early 1800s, some pioneers had started cattle ranches. They discovered that quarter horses had excellent "cow sense." This means the horses could work well with large herds. Ranchers bred the quarter horses with mustangs. This fast breed had arrived with Spanish colonists, though many ran free in the wild.

THE MANE FACT

After quarter horses were bred with mustangs, they became even stronger and livelier.

A Modern Work Horse

In 1940, the American Quarter Horse **Association** (AQHA) formed and gave the breed its official name. The association keeps records and offers training, education, and special events.

Ranchers today still use quarter horses to work with cattle. The horses can go places where ranchers' trucks can't. Mounted police officers in many cities ride these dependable horses, too.

Quarter horses are also used as **therapy** horses. Children learn to care for the horses and for themselves at the same time.

THE MANE FACT

There are over 5 million American quarter horse records in the American Quarter Horse Association!

This rancher uses a quarter horse, instead of a truck, to help move his herd down a hill.

13

Quarter horses are sometimes called the "world's fastest athletes."

A Racing Horse

Quarter horses race on short, straight tracks. The tracks are between 220 and 870 yards (201 and 796 m) long. There are about a hundred of these tracks in North America.

The quarter-horse race measuring 440 yards (402 m) is the most popular. Fans watch in excitement as the horses sprint down the track. Race times are measured to a hundredth of a second. The fastest horses finish the race in about 20 seconds. Their owners may win millions of dollars in prizes!

THE MANE FACT

The two biggest quarter-horse races each year take place in New Mexico and California. Races also take place in other parts of the world.

Quarter Horses for Fun

Have you ever been to a **rodeo** or another kind of horse show? If you have, you've seen quarter horses in action. They're skilled in events such as **barrel racing**, jumping, and cattle roping. Horses and their riders show off their skills in stopping, turning, and starting quickly.

Quarter horses are gentle and calm, so all ages can ride them. Some people own their horses, while others rent them from **stables**. There are riding trails all over the country.

Quarter horses are one of the most useful breeds in the world because they are skilled at so many tasks, including show jumping.

17

Hollywood quarter horses do tricks like standing up on their back legs, shaking their heads, and even playing dead!

18

Quarter Horses in the Movies

Quarter horses are easily trained, which makes them perfect for work in Hollywood. A quarter horse named Docs Keepin Time starred in *The Black Stallion* TV show and in the movies *Black Beauty* (1994) and *The Horse Whisperer* (1998). He's also made TV **commercials** and a music video!

In 2010, the movie *Secretariat* came out. It's about a racehorse superstar. Four Thoroughbreds played the role of Secretariat—and one quarter horse! The quarter horse, named Copper Locks, was used for the fastest racing scenes.

Keeping Quarter Horses Healthy

Quarter horses need fresh water and exercise daily. Most of the time, they eat hay. This breed gains weight quickly, so they shouldn't be given too much food. A grassy field is the perfect home for quarter horses. In cold or rainy weather, they like to wear blankets or stay in a barn.

A quarter horse's coat should be cleaned and brushed often. They should see an animal doctor, or veterinarian, for yearly checkups, shots, and teeth cleaning.

The Quarter Horse Timeline

1610	British colonists bring horses to Virginia. They breed their horses with Chickasaw Indian horses.
mid-1700s	Virginia farmers begin breeding English Thoroughbreds with colonial quarter horses.
late 1700s	Pioneers take quarter horses to the West.
1800s	Ranchers breed quarter horses with mustangs.
1860s	Pony Express riders use quarter horses.
1940	American Quarter Horse Association forms. The breed is officially named.
2011	More than 5 million records of American quarter horses have been collected by the American Quarter Horse Association.

Glossary

association: a group of people joined together for a purpose

barrel race: an event in which a horse and rider race in a certain path around objects

breed: a group of animals that share features different from other groups of the kind. Also, to choose which animals should come together to make babies.

commercial: a way of selling goods or services on TV or radio

hand: a measurement used for a horse's height. One hand equals 4 inches (10.2 cm).

mare: an adult female horse

pioneer: one of the first American settlers to travel to and settle in the West

rodeo: a contest of many events involving cowboy skills

sprint: to run fast for a short distance

stable: a building in which horses are kept

stallion: an adult male horse

therapy: a process of helping someone get better

For More Information

Books

Criscione, Rachel Damon. *The Quarter Horse.* New York, NY: PowerKids Press, 2007.

Landau, Elaine. *American Quarter Horses Are My Favorite!* Minneapolis, MN: Lerner, 2012.

Van Cleaf, Kristin. *Quarter Horses.* Edina, MN: ABDO Publishing Company, 2006.

Websites

American Quarter Horse Hall of Fame & Museum
www.aqha.com/Foundation/Museum.aspx
Take an online tour of the museum.

Quarter Horse
www.ansi.okstate.edu/breeds/horses/quarter/
Read about the history of quarter horses.

Publisher's note to educators and parents: Our editors have carefully reviewed these websites to ensure that they are suitable for students. Many websites change frequently, however, and we cannot guarantee that a site's future contents will continue to meet our high standards of quality and educational value. Be advised that students should be closely supervised whenever they access the Internet.

Index

American quarter horse 4, 5, 12, 21
American Quarter Horse Association (AQHA) 12, 21
barrel racing 16
Black Beauty 19
Black Stallion, The 19
breed 4, 5, 8, 11, 12, 17, 21
cattle 11, 12
cattle roping 16
Chickasaw Indians 8, 21
coat 7, 20
colonists 8, 9, 11, 21
colors 6, 7
Copper Locks 19
Docs Keepin Time 19
food 20
Hollywood 18, 19
Horse Whisperer, The 19
jumping 16, 17
mounted police officers 12
mustangs 11, 21
pioneers 11, 21
Pony Express 10, 21
racing 8, 15, 19
racing horse 7
ranchers 11, 12, 13, 21
riding trails 16
rodeo 16
Secretariat 19
show 16, 17
stock horse 7
therapy horses 12
Thoroughbreds 8, 19, 21
tracks 15
tricks 18
veterinarian 20